# HOW TO ORGANISE
# YOUR COMPUTER FILES

How To Organise Your Computer Files

by
Mark Sheeky

Pentangel Books

# How To Organise Your Computer Files

Written by Mark Sheeky.

Proofreading team headed by Deborah Edgeley.
With thanks to Bruce Mardle, Andrew Williams, and Chris Driver.

Illustrations and graphic design by Mark Sheeky.

1st edition, published in by Pentangel Books.
www.pentangel.co.uk
ISBN 978-1-9999800-6-1

Dedicated to cleaners, and forces of order
in all walks of life.

# CONTENTS

## INTRODUCTION

Welcome                                   1

## CHAPTERS

1. A Brief History of Computers           5
2. Files! Files!                          19
3. A Tree of Files                        27
4. Making a Start                         35
5. The Applications Folder                45
6. Sorting Everything Out                 57
7. The Dating Game                        63
8. Catalogues                             71
9. Current Buns                           79
10. Backing up                            85
11. Rules, and Breaking Them              97

## APPENDICES

Appendix 1: Diary Indexing                105
Appendix 2: Readable Date Format          111

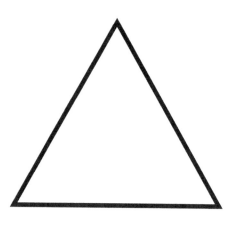

# Welcome

Welcome to the future, the joyous land of technology where our lives are made simple and efficient through the augmentation of machine-life to our crude and tired biology.

Alas, it can seem, at times, that computers make our lives more difficult and more complicated, rather than being the slick and easy-to-use promise that is the digital dream. But take heart! Like our organised and neat homes, and our organised and neat lives, it is easy to organise a computer; and your computer life can be made infinitely better with a few simple principles on how to file what and where.

We have reached a stage where the complexity of computers almost removes them from possible easy use by us mere humans. Rather than these machines either 'working' or 'not working', computers have now attained life-like properties of generally always being 'a little bit ill'.

Fortunately, we can work around this, and yes, even today, computers can be fantastic and perfect tools for our daily lives and jobs. With joy I can promise that even you can organise files in such a way that you'll know in an instant, and at any time, where a certain photo or document or video is saved; and you, in an instant, will know where your files should be saved so that you can access them at any time.

Prepare to be empowered!

# CHAPTER 1

# A BRIEF HISTORY OF COMPUTERS

# 1

# Start

Before we begin, I think it will be a good idea to share the history of my relationship with computers.

My love of computers, and the genesis of my logical mind, began at the innocent age of 11 years when my parents bought an ancient home computer for me, called a Dragon 32, in the early 1980s.

Home computers were plugged into ordinary television sets, and the Dragon 32 boasted 8 colours, most of which were green, and one of which actually made the television buzz (it was 'buff' - buzzy buff). I didn't see these dazzling colours for a few years because my first computer television was black and white. The delights of owning a black and white cathode-ray tube television will be forever beyond the people of today, just as the delights of using one of those old stick telephones are beyond all but the most ancient of us.

When the computer was turned on, it presented a curious and alluring flashing cursor. Typing any letter made letters appear, and anyone could simply type a command in its language and the machine would obey. This method of making a machine work still holds appeal. At times, wouldn't it be nice to just tell your computer, in plain English (or any other language) what you would like it to do?

The Dragon's language was BASIC[1], Microsoft BASIC, as it happens, and I learned how to program a few simple programs.

Computer magazines were eagerly collected from the newsagents, and these included program listings to copy from their pages. More advanced programs were written in 'machine code' - a raw list of numbers, usually in hexadecimal[2], which meant long hours typing number after number, not making one mistake. Each row of numbers had a 'check digit' at the end. This was a sum total of the line so that if you made a mistake you would have a clue about it and have the chance to retype the line. In this really slow, and very exacting way, some complex and fantastic computer games were typed in.

Back then, as I'm sure you know, computers used portable audio cassette recorders to store programs. Programs could be saved to a tape by typing the SAVE command, then pressing 'play and record' on the tape machine to make the spools roll, then pressing Enter to enact the command. The program was then saved out as a series of bleeps and blip sounds.

---

## BITS

Computers process and store everything as a list of zeros and ones called Bits. You can think of them as a row of lightbulbs, some on, some off. Eight bulbs in a row makes 256 possible combinations of pattern, from 00000000 to 00000001 to 00000010, and all the way up to 11111111. Counting in this way is called binary, a way of counting only using zero and one, compared to our usual decimal which is counting from zero to nine. A row of 8 binary lightbulbs like this is a byte.

---

## BYTES AND MEGABYTES

One thousand bytes is a kilobyte, or kB, colloquially known as 'K'. One million (1,000,000) bytes is a megabyte, MB, or 'meg'. One billion[3] (1,000,000,000) bytes is a gigabyte, GB, or 'gig'. One trillion[4] (1,000,000,000,000) bytes is a terabyte, TB (there isn't a common nickname for this yet!).

Now, sometimes these definitions can be twisted a little. In decimal, 1000 is a nice round number, but in binary 1024 is a round number (10000000000), so sometimes 1024 bytes can also be called a kilobyte. To end this confusion, 1024 bytes was renamed a kibibyte, and we also have mebibytes, gibibytes, tebibytes, etc.; but incorrect use of the powers-of-ten words still happens. Marketing people especially, those sneaky people, will sometimes use megabyte to mean a million bytes (correct!) or to mean mebibytes, just to make some fancy new device (a hard drive, memory, that sort of thing) seem bigger than it actually is.

You could save several programs in a row on one tape, like music tracks (yes, even music could be bought on cassette tape!). If your tape machine had a counter, you could note the number where the programs were and use fast-forward or rewind to get to the correct point. Without that you'd have to put everything at the start of a tape, which is wasteful for a long tape (I'm sure you remember, the biggest tapes used to store up to 45 minutes each side). These tape programs took a long time to load, sometimes 30 minutes or more. Smaller programs took less, perhaps 5 minutes. This is still a long wait by today's standards (although, hang on, we still wait a long time to upload and download films to YouTube. Perhaps times haven't changed). Loading and saving was precarious and not very reliable. Sometimes the tape would casually click off at the end and the computer still thought it was loading, its mind trapped in a hypnotic-bliss, the computer version of a day-dream.

Technology moved on. I upgraded to a Commodore 64 at some point, probably in the late 1980s. The C64 had a 'custom' tape recorder that came with it which was more reliable. My Dragon 32 tape machine was a Tandy tape recorder designed for home tape recording (and portable, it could use batteries). The Commodore 64 also had an optional disk drive, and my uncle, who was a computer technician, had one of these fantastic machines. The disk drive was huge, about the size of a shoe box, and used big flat disks, floppy disks, which, to my still-young self, were like the 'flexi-disc' music records which would occasionally come attached to the covers of magazines.

When using the computer, the disk drive was a revelation. Rather than fast forwarding or rewinding a tape to the correct point, programs could be saved or loaded at any time, and saving and loading was much faster.

I began to program a few simple games on the Commodore 64, and made a small tape of games for friends called The Laza Pack (in the 1980s it was cool to spell laser, or anything, with Zs). My games back then were programmed in BASIC again, albeit a slightly different version than that used by the Dragon.

Later, I started to learn 'machine code'. This, as on the Dragon, was a list of numbers and nothing more. One number meant 'store the next number'. One meant 'recall that number and add it to this', and things like that. So my machine code programs were just endless lists of numbers.

Then, I sold my beloved Commodore 64 and bought the next machine, an Amiga 500. This computer used a mouse, and an operating system called Workbench which was like today's[5] Microsoft Windows (or perhaps more like that used by Apple computers at the time, Apple Macintosh System 6). The Amiga had a built in floppy disk drive (joy!) but this time it used small disks which looked super futuristic. These 3.5″ disks (most computer hardware mysteriously avoided metric units) were both smaller and tougher, and another step more reliable, than the big floppy disks the Commodore 64 used.

When you turned on an Amiga, a picture of a hand inserting a disk appeared, a clue that you needed to insert one to get the computer to do anything. Workbench, the operating system, came on one disk. Put this in, and after a few clicks you were greeted to a blue screen and a red mouse arrow, and some windows. A few simple programs came with it. We might call these Apps now (short for Applications, a relatively modern term for a computer program).

## PIECES OF EIGHT, AND SIXTEEN

All computer data, and every single file, is nothing but a list of numbers stored as zeros and ones. Those 8 lightbulbs are 8 bits, and an 8-bit computer can access one byte in one go, so they can process numbers between 0 and 255 in a blink. Data rides around on motorways called buses, and an 8-bit computer has an 8-lane motorway.

A 16-bit computer can access 2 bytes in one go, it has a 16-bit bus. 16 bits can represent any number between 0 and 65535 (2 to the power of 16 means 65536 combinations), so 16-bit computers can process numbers between 0 and 65535 easily. A 32-bit computer can access 4 bytes in one go, so a number between 0 and 4,294,967,295... and so on. You can see how doubling the bit size leads to a much bigger number.

My Dragon 32, like most 1980s home computers, was an 8-bit machine, and the Amiga, like the Atari ST and the Sega Megadrive, was 16-bit[6]. Computers today are usually of the 64-bit size, so can process huge numbers, but history indicates that 128-bit, 256-bit, and perhaps even more, will eventually pop-up.

I programmed a bit more, this time using a language called Assembler, which, in essence, is like machine code but uses some short words to replace some numbers to make it easier to read. The Amiga also came with a version of BASIC, which was, again, based on Microsoft's version of BASIC, but it didn't work very well. With the Dragon 32 or the Commodore 64, you got the impression that you were command-ing the whole computer when you wrote a program. On the Amiga, programming in BASIC was like running something small in a corner while the rest of the computer 'did its own thing'. This was a sign of things to come.

I wrote a few simple games, and in the early 1990s I upgraded to an Amiga 1200. Now I had a built-in hard drive, which was something like a miracle at the time. When turning the com-puter on, it very quickly loaded the operating system, and there it was, without the need to insert any disks. The hard drive was super fast, huge in size compared to the floppy disks, and much more reliable. At some point in 1990s I bought a CD-Writer, and could magically save data (and music!) to a Compact Disc.

---

## MEMORIES OF THE OLDEN DAYS

The Dragon 32 had 32kB of memory.
The Commodore 64 had 64kB.
The Amiga 500 had 512kB, its disks held 880kB.
The Amiga 1200 had 2MB.
The space on a CD was a huge, for the time, 640MB.

A modern USB Flash Drive or SD Card can come in at 16GB without any problems, 128GB is closer to the norm at time of writing, and a contemporary hard drive is about 2TB.

---

By 1996 I had written a few games of dubious quality and, after writing 50 or so in my life up to that time, I had one published on Amiga by Vulcan Software. That game came on 6 floppy disks and had to be installed on a hard drive to work.

One thing about a hard drive is that it makes it easier to make backup copies of your important work in case of a disaster. On the Dragon 32, we could save a program to two tapes or more, if needed, or even (shock!) re-type the program in. On Amiga, we could save copies to extra floppy disks, or write the data to a CD. When a hard drive is there, its easy and blessedly fast to save a copy to a different folder on the hard drive.

I learned, though, that things can be lost. Hard drives are brilliant, but can break. The drive head hovers over the disk like a stylus over a record player; flying very low over it, the air gap is less than the width of a human hair, and the drive is spinning very quickly, up to 7200 revolutions per minute. By comparison, a vinyl record turns at a sleepy 45 RPM. A good washing machine on its spin cycle spins at 800 RPM, so the disk of a hard drive is spinning at nearly 10 times faster than a washing machine on spin, right next to a chunk of metal less than the width of a human hair away. Bear this delicacy in mind the next time you handle a hard drive.

The term 'crash' for a broken computer stems from the head literally crashing into the hard metal of the disk, a noisy calamity, but drives can and will fail naturally from all sorts of causes in the end. I've owned many computers and lots of different technology, so can recognise the signs of things 'getting old', starting to blink, click, and wobble on their metaphorical feet. Everything breaks eventually, this is why making backup copies of things are important, and part of the skill of this is knowing what to backup, and where.

My life crashed a little as my then-beloved Amiga computer, and my last big game project, came to an end in the late 1990s. In resignation, I sold the machine I'd spent my life mastering, and started again by buying an IBM-PC with a copy of Microsoft Windows 98. I started to learn C and C++ programming, and eventually made a few new games.

My PC seemed hugely complicated and over-engineered compared to the Amiga. Windows, for whatever reason, seemed to want people to do things in a certain way, but not a very good way. It never insisted; there were about eight ways of doing something, but in practice you had to dart between those paths to get any one thing done. It had silly ways of working which persist, such as sometimes clicking once on an icon or file to make it work, sometimes needing to do a double-click, and, in a surrealistic act, a slow double-click allowing to you rename the file.

The worst aspect of Windows is that it seems to deliberately hide how it works and what its doing behind many layers, such that even relative experts[7] can't really tell what is actually going on for most of the time. On my Amiga I used to simply switch it off when I'd finished and turn it on to start, like a regular television. My new and sparkly 1999 PC used to take forever to start and I'd have to 'shut it down' before even turning it off, and I had to ask permission to eject a disk or remove something.

But ho! This book isn't a critique of Windows (that would rival *War and Peace* in size); the principles here should apply to any computer system.

I started to learn to program on my PC, and I started to learn to file my creations. In 2002, frustrated at endless empty promises and stung by many scams, I decided to publish my own games and sell them online – the internet, a new world.

My old Amiga games had code numbers as well as titles, and this made it easier to add new games; how much more pleasing it is to put a book on the shelf when you have many empty shelves, each there waiting for each type of book. My Amiga game, Hilt II from 1996, for example, has code C18. I also started to record sound effects, and these collections of sounds were given code numbers too. Over the years, as I painted, wrote and published books, composed and published music, and organised live performance events, my filing systems expanded to cope with these new disciplines; each discipline coded with a letter and a number, and each item noted in an index containing basic details.

I've been typing, saving, loading, and filing computer files for over 30 years now, and have experienced enough crashes and failures to double check and future-proof everything – well, to try my best. My system of storing has evolved and refined slowly and steadily over that time, so perhaps now, in this late year of 2022, is the right time to write a book about organising computer files.

This book won't, at all, require you to go to great lengths to keep your computer neat. I wanted to write a guide, not a manual; to share how I've learned to do things. You can take from it as much or as little as you want, but hopefully, by the end of it, you'll know where to store what, and where to find it again when you need to.

Let us begin.

## NOTES

1. BASIC stands for Beginners' All-purpose Symbolic Instruction Code, and is an easy to use and easy to learn programming language.
2. Hexadecimal, or hex, is a base-16 number system, as opposed to the base-10 system we are used to. Hex counts using digits 0 to 9, then A to F; so 00, 01, etc. then 09, 0A, 0B etc. up to FF, which equates to 255 in decimal. Hex numbers, when written, typically start with '0x' to indicate the number is hex; so 'FF' would be written '0xFF'.
3. 1,000,000,000 is an American billion. In Britain, a billion used to mean a million million (1,000,000,000,000) but partly due to computers, 1,000,000,000 is pretty much now the global standard.
4. Again, 1,000,000,000,000 is an American trillion, which is the most common meaning of trillion nowadays.
5. in 2022.
6. The bus widths in different parts of a computer can vary, so the Dragon had some 8-bit and some 16-bit parts; the Amiga had 16-bit and 32-bit parts.
7. There are no actual experts in Microsoft Windows, its complexity has grown beyond complete human comprehension. I am far from an expert, and if anyone tells you that they are, they either know that they aren't and are lying, or think that they are and are a buffoon!

# CHAPTER 2

# FILES! FILES!

# 2

Welcome to the world of files. What types of files have we got?

## Data!

We have data files which are: Documents (this generally means text files or written things), Images (pictures/photos), Videos, Music (and sound effects!), System or Config Files which control or inform other programs (these are sometimes secret things, sometimes things we can control); and Others, like special file types saved out by specific programs. Sometimes there are crossovers... like a 'gif', those short looping animations we see on the internet... are they Images or Videos? Is a flyer an Image or a Document?

Generally a data file is associated with a program. An image file might be associated with an image viewer, for example. The operating system determines these associations, and therefore what sort of file is what. Windows does this based mainly on the extension in the filename. '.docx', for example, means a Word Document, and '.jpg' means a jpeg image.

## Programs

There are also Programs (Software, Apps, or Applications, we'll always call them programs), which are generally installed somewhere by the system. You can put and move any file to anywhere you like, and in the old and happy days even programs could be moved around anywhere; but now you generally can't move programs. Programs these days are often bundles of files, with at least one main file that is executed[1] and other files that it may need or want. When installing programs you have some control over where they are put.[2]

Computers now try to separate data files from programs for security reasons, so they try to keep programs in one place and data in another. This is not always helpful because almost all programs need to access some data files. It doesn't particularly help security either, the main security problem comes from data files (such as things that appear to be documents or images) that have secret programs inside (sneaky!).

We also have Setup Programs, Installers or Package files to install a new program. These are programs that unpack themselves, and like an unfolding magical suitcase, they open up to form a circus-tent full of wonders.

## Signs

There are also Shortcuts (known as Aliases on MacOS), which are small files which point to another. You can think of these as signposts pointing the way to another file, and when you click on it, you instantly jump to the file it is pointing to. In the vast countryside of your computer, you might want to drop a signpost.

Shortcuts can be confusing because it's all too easy to forget that something is a shortcut, or not know where the file it is pointing to actually IS. Deleting a Shortcut won't delete the file, it's more like destroying the signpost that points to it.

Likewise, sending someone a Shortcut is like handing them a big wooden arrow, one that points to a distant place on someone else's computer.

Shortcuts are most useful on the Desktop, Start Menu or similar place to instantly open a program which could be anywhere. For us archivists, they are best avoided.

---

## THE LONG AND THE SHORTCUTS

Windows has a few 'super-shortcuts' built-in. 'Desktop', 'Downloads', 'Documents', 'Music', 'Pictures', 'Videos' jump straight to folders in the system 'Users' folder for the current user. They can't be edited or moved or deleted like normal shortcuts, they're like magical portals that exactly reflect the contents of the user folders.

---

## Folders & Zips

We have folders, which are like empty drawers to store our files in. Before windows-based operating systems, these were called Directories. Folders are your friend. These are the key and magical way to organise your computer. A good general principle is the Golden Rule Number 1:

## GOLDEN RULE NUMBER 1
A folder should contain <u>only</u> files or <u>only</u> folders.

We will come back to this later.

Finally there are Compressed Files which can be anything: data or a program. Windows and MacOS have zip-file support built in. Any file ending in '.zip' is a pile of other files squashed into one, a proverbial suitcase of stuff. This can be really useful, but remember that this is one file and that when we look inside we are just opening our suitcase a crack and seeing what is inside. It's not quite as fast or as easy to move files around in zip files as it is to move files in folders.

There are other types of compressed file too, not just zip. '.7z' files are one, for example. The Amiga used '.lha' files. Most of those need another program to open (or 'unpack' or 'decrunch') them. These other types are rare these days, so it's not something to be worried about.

## OPERATING SYSTEMS

When it comes to viewing and manipulating files, Windows and MacOS have become pretty similar.

On Windows Windows+E opens Windows Explorer, and on Mac Command+N opens with Mac equivalent, Finder.

To Cut, Copy, or Paste a file, or anything else (like some selected text), use Ctrl+X, Ctrl+C, Ctrl+V on Windows, and Command+X, Command+C, Command+V on MacOS.

## NOTES

1. Some deadly terms: 'Executed' means a program is started, its instructions are enacted. This process is very like pushing the first domino in a row of toppling dominoes, which is why the word is so dramatic. If a program or process is 'terminated' or 'killed' it means that it's stopped by an external force. A program that 'dies' stops itself, unintentionally. 'Dead' computers are usually broken and unresponsive.
2. "When installing programs you have some control over where they are put"... is something I've written with a hint of irony. In the early days, I used to install graphics programs in a folder called Graphics; sound programs in a folder called Sound, and so forth. Gradually, things stopped working correctly and occasional problems began to creep in, so now I simply install everything to its preferred location. Much as I'd love to order every part of the computer, this book must be about how to organise your files. We will let system files and programs take care of themselves.

HOW TO

# CHAPTER 3

# A TREE OF FILES

# 3

Welcome to a world of neatness. Now that the basics are out of the way, we can start to arrange the chaos of our computer world. First, we need to divide up files into the different categories that we might use.

You can think of your computer like a house, and folders like rooms. On a cluttered computer you have one big room, and books and toys and all sorts of things are piled up everywhere. In an ordered computer we start in an empty chamber with white walls, and a few doors. These lead to other rooms, also bare, empty and with a few doors. As we go through each door, the rooms get smaller each time until we find a cupboard with just one type of thing inside. This is the ideal of order.

This structure is known as a tree because it has a few core 'trunks' which split into a few more branches, getting finer and finer as needed.

## THE RULE OF LESS THAN TEN

There is both a belief and some research[1] that people can relatively easily remember up to seven things, plus or minus two, or in other words, less than ten. This is a good rule to organise your world by, and when making your computer tree, try to limit the number of different branches at any junction to less than ten; so on a computer you might start with seven folders, each with seven inside, and so on.

Now, sometimes a folder will have hundreds of other folders or files inside, I have some with thousands, but when that happens they all tend to be one type of thing.

It's less than ten *different* things, options, that should be our maximum. Have you ever been to a fancy ice-cream parlour with 40 flavours on show? How hard is it to choose a flavour? Things are more efficient when you only have a few choices.

If we're at a junction in the road of our computer life, it's op-timal to have less than ten choices. If you find you have 20 or 30 different folders in one, try to slim them down into a few broad categories.

We'll build some basic folders in a moment, first let's establish how folders and paths look on various computers, and in this book.

Let's start with a blank drive. It has one folder called 'Images' on it. 'Images' has one folder inside called 'Artworks', and 'Artworks' contains one folder called 'Archive'. Archive is empty. An MS-DOS or Windows file path describing this looks like this:

C:\Images\Artworks\Archive\

The C is the base drive and backslashes separate the folders. Back in the olden days A and B were floppy drives, which is why things still don't tend to start with A.

Mac OS (and Unix and Linux) use forward-slashes, like this:

/Images/Artworks/Archive/

And the internet uses forward-slashes too (I'm cheating a bit here because many websites have a '.com' in them or something like that, but you get the idea):

https://Images/Artworks/Archive/

---

## SLASH AND GRAB

Whether there is an \ or / at the end of a path doesn't tend to matter[2], but it's a good idea to put one there because it makes it clear that 'Archive', in the above examples, is the last folder in the chain, and not a file called Archive. As I'm sure you know, files often have a dot extension, like '.jpg' for a jpeg image; so when you see a file called 'Picture.jpg', you know it's an image file, and computers guess this too. So, you can generally tell a file from a folder this way – but it's not always obvious. Windows, by default, hides these extensions (bah!). On Amiga, files often lacked extensions.

So, if you should ever write a file path, keep a slash at the end.

---

In this book I'll use arrows, like this:

'Images → Artworks → Archive'

This is because slashes can be used in writing (as I'm sure you notice and/or realise), so it's better to use an explicit symbol. These will always be paths in this book, there are no filenames at the end. I will enclose the path in single quotes to make the path explicit rather than appending a slash.

Another way of viewing paths is a tree-like structure, like this:

▷Images
→▷Artworks
→→▷Archive

I will be using this form too. This makes it visually clear that Archive is inside Artworks. which is inside Images. To make any new folders stand out, I'll sometimes use grey text for existing folders. Here, for example, is a new folder called Photos in Images:

▷Images
→▷Artworks
→→▷Archive
→▷Photos

NOTES

1. The Magical Number Seven, Plus or Minus Two: Some Limits on our Capacity for Processing Information by George A. Miller, (1956).
2. Try visiting 'https://www.google.com' vs. 'https://www.google.com/'.

HOW TO

# CHAPTER 4

# MAKING A START

# 4

Let's build some basic folders. Create these folders in your root drive. This root could be your base drive (such as C: in Windows), your Documents folder, or wherever you want to put everything:

▷Applications
▷Audio
▷Images
▷Video
▷Temporary
▷Text

This is a basic set that will suit just about every computer user. It's mostly obvious what we will put in them, which is a good sign.

What goes in the Applications folder, however, isn't so obvious. This will contain setup programs, installers, and that sort of thing. It will be our archive of setups. It will contain things that you'll probably use just once, but we'll keep a copy here, just in case.

Audio will contain music and anything sound based, and Images, and Video[1] will contain those things.

Text will contain, well, text-based files. The word Documents is often used to mean this, but a 'document' to me evokes something like a newspaper article that might include images or fancy layouts. I wanted to choose a word that was explicitly text-based. You'll note I've called it 'Text' not 'Texts'. To match the convention of using plurals here, we should really call this 'Texts', but that word is a bit of a tongue twister[2], so for ease, we'll stick with 'Text' instead.

Temporary will generally be empty, and used for anything, well, temporary. You might need an empty folder to put something in for a short while, and that's what this is for. I use Temporary folders quite a lot.

I haven't abbreviated anything so that it's easy to read. Ease of reading, and ease of understanding are important, but so is keeping things short and neat. We need to remain on guard to be efficient at both.

This is our base, the six doors in our start room. We might need more (websites, anyone?), and we will look at those in a moment, but first...

## Temporary Secretary

There are a few more standard folders that we can create, which I use a lot. We've already created one root folder called 'Temporary'; this is like the entrance hall, the porch, of our computer. It will often be empty, but you might want to put something you're working on in there.

After years of using computers, I find it's very helpful to have a few of these, so, create a folder named 'Temporary' inside Audio. Create another inside Images, another inside Text, and another inside Videos; all called 'Temporary'.

Now everything looks like this (I've made the existing folders grey to make these new ones stand out):

▷Applications
▷Audio
→▷Temporary
▷Images
→▷Temporary
▷Videos
→▷Temporary
▷Temporary
▷Text
→▷Temporary

Sometimes I'll be working on an image, and will crop it or toy with it before, say, uploading to social media, or emailing it to someone. I'm not going to want to keep it forever, so I'll save it into Temporary images. The same is true of audio; I might download a music clip, or take a short recording and want to save it somewhere to look at and decide if I want to keep it. In that case I'll put this in the Temporary audio folder. If I'm making a film, it is the Temporary video folder where I put the raw camera footage before sorting it out, deciding what to keep or discard.

I find it really useful to separate Temporary folders for images, audio, video, and text like this. If I had just one Temporary folder, it could become too large, with a mix of different data. One purpose of a temporary folder is to have a blank, clean space to view a few related files in one glance.

Having a few Temporary folders also makes it easier to work out what to put where: when taking photos from your camera, put them all in 'Images → Temporary'. Then you can take a look and decide where to file them (or what to delete).

Use your Temporary folders as much as you like. Aim to keep them empty, so delete everything in there after you've used them, or, if you want to keep something, file it in the correct place. The items in Temporary are for examination and sorting. You'll either move (or send) them somewhere else, or decide you don't want them and will delete them.

## Adding More

We've made a good start but we might want to create some more folders.

Perhaps you are an author and want somewhere to file your books. If so, create a folder called Books. Where would you put that? That's right, the Text folder seems ideal. You might be a journalist and want to file your articles, so creating an Articles folder in Text would be a good idea too.

If you are a visual artist, creating a folder called Artworks might be a good idea, and the Images folder seems like a good place for that.

As a computer programmer, I need a place to file my programs in development. Now, computer programs have some elements of text, but also some images, and some sounds. Our current folders like Text or Images or Audio don't seem quite right for this mix. For situations like this, it's best to create a new root folder, so, on my computer I have a 'Programming' folder in the root for that[3].

Websites are another example of a mix of files and file types. If you have a website or two, a root folder named 'Websites' is a good idea, with a new folder inside for each website. If you've designed the site from scratch yourself, those contents could mirror the exact site you have online. Increasingly, website design is an online, and somewhat hidden activity. It can be tempting to log-in and design, monitor, and update your website online and never trouble yourself to download any of it or worry about how it works. If this is you, all you might need or want are some images which you could store in the Images folder; but even then it is a good idea to occasionally download a copy of your website, which is usually an option. If you design websites, your core data will probably be in an SQL database, which you can, and ideally should, download regularly. A 'Databases' folder inside 'Websites' is a good place to keep a copy of these.

I also store Events as a new folder in the root. Events for me include music performances, competitions, art exhibitions and various star-spangled and glittery occasions like that. These too are a mix of images, video, audio, text; and so a new folder of their own works best; so I have 'Events' in the root, too.

So, it's time to think about what you want and need to store. Create some folders for those and put them in the place you think makes most sense.

Remember, our folder names like Audio, Images, Text are labels to help us remember what is where. If you have filed away your holidays... where would you look to find them? Holidays might include photos, videos, and written plans, so a new folder called Holidays might be best... but you might think of holidays as visual, perhaps they are 90% photos, and so you might prefer to put the Holidays folder in Images.

Do what makes most sense to you.

Don't worry about making everything perfect right away. Your computer will constantly change and evolve, and its easy to rename and move things around later.

On the right, see a full tree of the folders I've talked about:

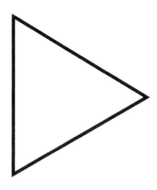

▷Applications
▷Audio
→▷Temporary
▷Events (optional!)
▷Holidays (optional!)
▷Images
→▷Artworks (optional!)
→▷Temporary
▷Programming (optional!)
▷Videos
→▷Temporary
▷Temporary
▷Text
→▷Articles (optional!)
→▷Books (optional!)
→▷Temporary
▷Websites (optional!)

Remember to try to keep the number of folders at any branch below ten, if possible. We're pushing at that limit already. We could, for example, put Holidays and Events together in a new folder (Activities?).

## NOTES

1. Now that 'a video' is a thing, the word 'Videos' is considered a valid plural, but like 'Audio', I prefer to use the word Video.
2. Pope Sixtus the Sixth's Six Texts.
3. Calling the folder 'Programs' would more closely match the naming convention of the other folders, but it might become confused with actual programs rather than our programming creations.

# CHAPTER 5

# THE APPLICATIONS FOLDER

5

The Applications folder is something of a special area, so we'll jump in there now. It can become more haphazard than our ordered world because things like setup programs, device drivers, and games can be named in all sorts of ways and sometimes even (shudder!) be more than one file.

We'll deal with that here.

Create these 7 folders in Applications. Generally these will correspond to types of software, and again tend to be similar for everyone:

▷Applications
→▷Audio
→▷FileSystem
→▷Games
→▷Graphics
→▷Internet
→▷Science
→▷Text

Remember, we'll be putting setup programs here, but it won't all be software. Sometimes programs need extra data that is installed or unpacked elsewhere, and that goes here too. This can include things like fonts, sample-libraries, plug-ins (for audio or graphic software), game levels, system drivers, language packs, and that sort of thing. All of the Applications folders will contain things that we might rarely use, perhaps install once and may never need again, but we are self-sufficient super-humans with a wonderful computer toolkit, so we like to keep copies of this sort of thing, just in case, don't we?

Audio will be for music editors, or any software that is sound based, like the sound editor for your Yamaha Synthesizer. Create a folder in Audio called Software. If you use audio plug-ins, soundfonts, sample libraries, or similar things, you might want to create a suitable folder here for those.

FileSystem will be for system drivers, computer tools, and software for testing, repairing or monitoring the computer system. Examples are CD writer software, anti-virus software, disk repair tools, backup software, and file compressors and decompressors. Create two folders in FileSystem: one called Software and one called Drivers.

---

## THE SPACES BETWEEN US

You will notice in this book that I don't use spaces in my names of folders and files. My folder 'FileSystem' isn't, for example, 'File System'. Computers have allowed spaces in file and folder names for years, but I really like to know when a name starts and ends. You can, for example, quite legally make a file called 'This      Is My          Song.mp3', which is certain to cause confusion at some point.

For me, removing spaces aids my reading, but there's no technical reason to exclude spaces, so feel free to use spaces if you prefer.

---

Games are where we will store any game setups. Sometimes games nowadays are stored online and downloaded and updated in secret, but it's still useful to have a space to put any game setups if we need to, as well as things like updates, patches, or extras. Back when I used to buy games in boxes on CD (ah, memories!) I would copy the Setup.exe from the CD into here. Create a folder in Games called Software. If you have bonus game material, such as extra levels, mods, texture packs, and things like that, you might want to create a folder for those ('Updates' perhaps?). I also have a folder called Emulation here, for games for other computer systems.

Graphics is for any graphic or video software, from paint programs to video editors, to 3D animation systems. The latter example indicates why, unlike in our main filing system, the Graphics folder works best when it covers both images and videos. Graphics programs often blur the two. We will also save fonts here. Fonts tend to be installed on the computer, so you might want to keep a separate copy of any new and fancy fonts that you download. Create two folders in Graphics: one called Software and one called Fonts. If you have plug-ins, texture packs, clip-art, or other graphics related content, then create some appropriate folders for those, too. Sometimes clip-art or libraries of images aren't 'installed' in a technical sense, they may simply be a compressed folder of image files, but if it's something I've downloaded, particularly if paid for, then I like to keep a compressed copy of the original file, and this is the place to keep it.

Internet is for internet or communications software; things like

FTP programs, web browsers, and website designers. Create a folder in Internet called Software for these programs. Apart from 'Software', you might want a folder for things like web-browser plug-ins or language packs.

Science is for maths, science, or other technical software that doesn't quite fit into other categories. This will include calculators and maths software, astronomy and molecular-biology software, simulation and/or engineering software. This is a somewhat specialised folder, but software like this doesn't really fit into the other categories; if the Text folder is the English department of your computer school then the Science folder is the Maths department. Create a folder in Science called Software. What might need to go here that isn't Software? Perhaps extra content, plug-ins, or other data used by this specialised software.

Finally, Text is for text editors and other writing software. Create a folder in Text called Software. If you have different language packs for your text editors, then you might want to create a suitable folder for those. As an author, I keep my barcodes and ISBN codes in a folder here. As with image clip-art, these aren't strictly 'installed' anywhere, but this is the ideal place to keep a compressed copy of these assets.

## SECRET BUTLERS

These days, a lot of software is downloaded secretly somewhere and automatically installed. Drivers are a perfect example, these are rarely seen and sometimes (shudder!) can't be updated or changed anyway.

Sometimes a setup program, particularly one for anti-virus software and web browsers, is a tiny thing which doesn't contain the program at all. These act like little portals that connect to the internet and download the 'latest version' when installing.

This trend will probably increase, but there are plenty of programs that do still have complete setups.

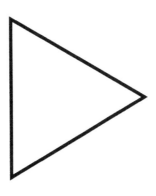

Your Applications folder should now look like this (I've made the existing folders grey to highlight the new ones):

▷Applications
→▷Audio
→→▷Software
→▷FileSystem
→→▷Drivers
→→▷Software
→▷Games
→→▷Software
→▷Graphics
→→▷Fonts
→→▷Software
→▷Internet
→→▷Software
→▷Science
→→▷Software
→▷Text
→→▷Software

Now, when you download something, you can save it to the correct place to keep a copy. If you buy a new computer, you'll have a copy of everything to install, and you'll have copies of software to give to friends if needed. If you download a font, you can save it to 'Applications → Graphics → Fonts' and from there install that and still keep a copy.

For any hardware drivers, save those to 'FileSystem → Drivers'. Drivers are usually secretly downloaded and automatically installed by the operating system, but you can, if you ever wanted or needed to, find drivers online to download, too. Even today, some hardware comes with a driver on a flash drive or CD. If so, it is a good idea to copy that over to your Drivers folder, to have a backup.

Years ago, the Applications folder was really useful to me. Now almost everything is online, and it can be better to search for the latest version of something online rather than use an old installer... but not always. Sometimes a newer thing won't work when an older version did, and older versions of things have a habit of vanishing from the internet forever. Sometimes good software, which was and still is, perfectly good, simply vanishes from the internet altogether, so it's always useful to keep copies of these things.

---

## NAMES...

There isn't a standard naming convention for setup programs, and they can be quite obscure and confusing. Irfanview, the marvellous image viewer for Windows, version 4.60, is named 'iview460_setup.exe'. Version 7.3.2 of LibreOffice is named 'LibreOffice_7.3.2_Win_x86.msi'.

---

## ...AND DREAMS

At one time, I dreamt of renaming everything to match a standard, with the program name and the version. The Irfanview setup would be named 'Irfanview-v460.exe' and everything would look neat and be joyous. Sadly, as you can see, LibreOffice has three digits in the version (should we include dots?) and the name also has alternative Operating System versions (Win_x86). Some programs have languages in the filename, too (like 'en-GB'), or they can be a seemingly random gaggle of numbers ('WG111v3_v2.0.0_Setup.exe' - I'm looking at you! - notice how this has two version numbers in there, too).

Another downside to renaming setups is that it can, ironically, make it harder to compare a file with a different version of the same program. At least if you keep the original file name you can (well, *should* be able to) see any differences. So, I decided to just keep files named as they come.

THE APPLICATIONS FOLDER

HOW TO

# CHAPTER 6

# SORTING EVERYTHING OUT

6

So now we have a few empty folders and, by their name, have an idea what to put in them.

For many uses, this is already enough. Let's say we have a new fancy MP3 Player and we have 100 '.mp3' files for it. Where would we put those?

Somewhere in Audio makes sense. We could create a new folder in Audio called 'MP3Player' and put all of the files in there. They are all the same type of file, so they should all be pretty easy to browse and view. There might be quite a few files but we should be able to keep track of them. We should be careful to name them in some meaningful way... perhaps we could name them after the artist and song title[1].

To go further we could, if we wanted, make a folder for each album, or perhaps one for the artist, 'Sparks', then the album title inside, 'Propaganda', then put each file from that album in there. This is how Amazon Music currently organise things; although, if we are copying these to an MP3 Player, we might note that not all MP3 Players will recognise folders like this.

---

## TAG CITY

MP3 files include Tags, extra data in the file; in this case things like song name, album name, artist name, music genre, etc. MP3 Players will generally look there for this informa-tion and index everything based on that – they will ignore the filenames, seeking only the tags with vampiric avarice.

---

You can get special tag editors to edit these data.

JPG files include tags too, data like camera make and model, and all sorts of things. Tags are creeping their way into every file for various reasons, but the name of the file itself is still the best way to identify it, so try to keep filenames meaningful. Bear in mind that files love to be sorted alphabetically.

Let's look at another example. We've just set up a website and we want somewhere to keep all of the images we are using for it. The Images folder seems like the perfect place, so we create a folder in there called 'Websites', and another inside called 'MyWebsite' and put all of our images in there. We've put it in Images because we're mostly using images (well, duh). If you're including HTML code, or want to store lots of other types of files too, it might be a better idea to create a 'Websites' folder in the root rather than in Images.

Your aim in all things should be ease of use, to put files where you would first look for them.

So, we already have enough types of folder for casual use, but there are some occasions when we could do better.

Let's pretend we've been out for a nice day and taken a few photos. Where do we put them? Yes, that's right, somewhere in Images. We could create a new folder called Photos, couldn't we? But... we can't just dump a lifetime of photos in there... this is something that will grow to be huge over the years, and digital photos have a habit of having obscure names

('SDC10719.JPG', anyone?).

We could create a new folder for each day trip. This is better, but, what if, in ten years time and after 500 day trips, we want to find this one day? What is the best option?

Also, photos are an easy case. What if we design cakes for a living. Where do we file our Cake designs so that we can find and manage them all neatly? Unlike the photos of a day trip, the date of our cake design might not be as important, and we might want to update or change it over the years.

For well-ordered archives like this, we file our things only in two ways: by date, and by catalogue.

Turn the page to explore filing by date...

NOTES

1. I name my MP3 files by artist name (arranged alphabetically), hyphen, album title, hyphen, two-digit track number, hyphen, and track name. Each word starts with a capital letter. Here is an example: 'WakemanRick-JourneyToTheCentreOfTheEarth-26-HallOfTheMountainKing.mp3'. Without going into pedantic depth, note that on computers, as far as filenames are concerned, the minus and the hyphen are effectively the same.

HOW TO

# CHAPTER 7

# THE DATING GAME

# 7

I file photos by date. In 'Images → Photos' I have lots of folders, each named simply after a year '2000', '2001', '2002', etc. This means that, when I list the folders alphabetically, the years will naturally flow from past to present. It makes it relatively easy to track down a particular day. When New Year's Day comes around, I just create a new folder for the new year.

For some types of file this is enough, an entire year's worth of files can go into one folder. Whether this works depends on how manageable the results are for you; how many files you have in there, and how easy it is for you to find them. In my Text folder, I file 'Notes' by year in this way. In there I have all sorts of small text files, from ideas for concept albums to letters I've sent. There aren't that many files over a year, so this is manageable, and I tend to name similar files with the same few letters at the start, so that when I order everything alphabetically, similar files are naturally grouped together.

Any letters, for example, I name 'LetterToJohnSmith.doc'. The 'LetterTo' bit at the start groups all of the documents together, and I only write about two per year, so they're easy to find.

For Photos though, you might want to organise these further because even a year's worth of photos can be a lot, and you might want to separate different events or days out. Again, filing by date is a good way.

Do this by creating a new folder for each day trip. This should also begin with a date, but a two-digit number this time, 01 for January, to 12 for December. I then use the month name, because it makes it easier to identify the month (you might be the sort of person who thinks... '04... aha! April!', in which case you can skip this). I then name the event.

## SORT ME OUT

The fact that files are easily viewed alphabetically makes the name the ideal way to order them. Get into the habit of naming files and folders from the start. This way, a file called 'LetterToJohnSmith.doc' would naturally appear grouped with 'LetterToBob.doc' and 'LetterToZoe.doc', in a list, where as 'BobsLetter.doc' might be miles away from 'ZoesLetter.doc' because every file between B and Z would be in-between.

When it comes to numbers, beware! Note that there are two different ways files are sorted. Sometimes, particularly with older systems, a file named 'Name10.doc' would annoyingly appear before 'Name1.doc'. Often nowadays, 'Name1.doc' does appear before 'Name10.doc', but not always. When using numbers, a good way to do it is to add zeros to the start to make the number the same number length, so use 'Name01' rather than 'Name1'. This is called padding. Alphabetically, 'Name01.doc' will always appear before 'Name10.doc'.

If you only need a few digits, such as the numbers 1 to 12 for months, it will look neater and work more consistently to pad the numbers and use 01 to 12. Back in ye-olde days of computers it was reasonably common to see files named 'File00000123.tif' for this reason.

I still use these padded numbers at times, but more than four zeros in a row becomes difficult to read: 0000000 vs. 000000 can easily be confused, so I use plain numbers most of the time, and remain grateful that today's computers tend to sort these correctly.

So in Photos I have a folder named '12-Dec-Birthday' and all birthday photos go in there. I can also have '12-Dec-Christmas' as a separate folder. Putting the two-digit month first will automatically sort things from old to new. If you wanted to take things to another level, you can put the year first too, like '2020-12-Dec-Birthday'. This would match the arrangement of the ISO Standard for dates (yay!), and allow you to copy one folder into one from another year without a clash; but you may consider this overkill. One reason for putting everything in a year folder is that you already know what year the contents are from.

So, we have a nice way to file things neatly by date. This works brilliantly for Photos, Holidays, or any regular accumulation of files that you want to keep a record of.

Now, photos is a broad subject, but you can use the same system to be more specific with your subjects. Would you search for a holiday under 'Germany' or under '2007'? If the former, you could choose to file under 'Holidays → Germany → 2007'. If the latter you could use 'Holidays → 2007 → 01-Jan-Germany'.

---

## THINGS I FILE BY DATE

Holiday photos (yay!).

Written 'Notes', which includes letters, ideas, invoices I might send, or anything I type and want to keep.

'Documents', which for me means anything text-based that I've been sent that I want to keep. This includes receipts and bills, flyers, newsletters. Generally anything I want to keep that I haven't written myself.

I file my music by year. This is perhaps odd. You might imagine a record collection to be filed by music artist or something like that, but my 'Audio → Music' folder contains lots of different formats and types of music, often by friends or created by myself. I have MIDI files, and MOD files, and SID files from decades ago, and this includes over 200 Amiga and C64 music artists, who often have just one tune to their name – but all from the same year, and (sadly) rarely revisited; so it makes sense for me to file music by year.

---

Filing my 'Notes' by month is not ideal because I might not remember when I wrote that Letter to John Smith. I could create a folder 'Letters' inside my year folder, that would work.

In my case, I can see a year's worth of Notes in a glance, so it's more efficient to put everything in one year folder.

If in doubt you can file everything by year, it works especially well for files you will regularly accumulate over time. It stops one folder growing too huge, and sorts your files into neat bunches.

Another nice thing about date filing is that it makes annual backups really easy. New things can go into the current year, and you can generally forget about older years, except when looking for older things. This makes it instantly clear what is new, and what needs to be backed up, and what is old, and has already been backed up.

Date filing works well for things which slowly grow over time, but if you use your computer for work there might be better a way to file things. You might have older projects that you revisit every so often, and semi-active projects in previous years might be both harder to find, and easier to miss when you update them. If you do update your fancy new cake design, should it go back into the 1989 folder, or this year?

This is where catalogue filing comes in.

# HOW TO

# CHAPTER 8

# CATALOGUES

8

Catalogue filing is simply a way to file everything so that we can find it easily. The principle is that everything has a number and a name, rather than using the date.

Let's go back to that idea of a cake design business. We've created a Cakes folder in Images, and we've made a clown cake design, and a cake that looks like a steam train, 'Train Cake', too. We put photos and recipes of our designs in these folders. So our computer looks like this now (I will omit the other folders, like Applications, Audio, Temporary etc.):

▷Images
→▷Cakes
→→▷ClownCake
→→→▷(lots of picture files and details of the clown cake)
→→▷TrainCake
→→→▷(lots of picture files and details of the train cake)

Essentially, this is how catalogue filing works.

But we can make it even better. One problem with this is that folders are generally sorted alphabetically. Adding a new 'Easter Cake' will shove it in between ClownCake and TrainCake, so it might not be instantly obvious that the Easter Cake is a recent creation. You can (usually) sort and view folders by date, but this isn't always reliable because dates have a habit of changing at unexpected times. Also, what if you created two Clown Cakes?

A good solution is to give each cake design a number, and start the folder name with that number. For things like this I also use a letter. A common letter or word at the start makes it clear from that code alone that we're talking about a cake rather than it being any old number.

Let's use C, for cake, as an example. So we would name our folders:
C1-ClownCake
C2-TrainCake

If you make a new Easter Cake, that can be C3-EasterCake, and a new Clown Cake can be C4-ClownCake. Now everything looks neat and orderly. New cakes will go naturally on the end of the line, and the list can keep growing neatly for as long as we keep baking.

Even without anything more, the C-number codes in the name have already made things look and work neater.

But we can still go further. If we want, we can write somewhere, in a separate list, what sort of cake C1 and C2 is. Doing this is really useful. Firstly, it gives you a chance to write some extra details about each cake (when you made it, what the recipe was, etc.) all in one index file. If this interests you, see Appendix 1 (p. 104) for an example of an index diary entry.

There is nothing more to my catalogue system than this.

# C FOR CAKE

There are a few variations of code–number–name.

Rather than 'C1-ClownCake', you could use 'Cake1-ClownCake', or 'Cake 1 – Clown Cake', or pad the number to make it a consistent length: 'Cake0001-ClownCake'. Some people use underscores ('_') instead of hyphens, but they can appear confusing in a list and are harder to line up visually. Dots can become confused with file types, so they are best avoided, too. See how:
Cake 1 . Clown Cake.jpg
looks more ethereal than:
Cake0001-ClownCake.jpg

Padding the number usually looks neater, but you need to make sure you don't run out of numbers. Are you ever likely to make more than 10,000 cakes? If I pad numbers at all, I limit it to four, 0000, or less. More than that can be eye-boggling and cause accidental mistakes.

For my old YouTube programme, ArtSwarm, I name episodes 'ArtSwarm-S1E001-EndingAndBeginnings', for example. There are less than 10 series, and less than 1000 episodes per series, so one digit for Series, and three for Episode is fine, and everything lines up and sorts neatly.

I apply this system for just about everything I create, from this very book, to my paintings and artworks, to my music, and the software I program.

# Work in Progress

There is one final tweak we can make. This system works great for filing finished work, but it can be useful to separate the things we are working on from the completed projects in our long-term archive. For everything I file in the catalogue way, I create two folders, always named the same: 'Archive', and 'Inuse'.

Archive

This is for finished projects. In our example, all of our cakes will be filed in here.

Inuse

This will contain things we are working on now.

Incidentally, you might prefer to use 'InUse' instead, and indeed, the guidelines here have recommended this form of capitalisation ('Camel Case'). To me it looks visually neater to use one short word, 'Inuse', so I've evolved, over the years, to prefer that. Inuse has become a new word in my mental vocabulary to mean an active work project.

So, if we go back to the cake designs example, and pretending that we did make that second clown cake, our folders will look like this:

▷Images
→▷Cakes
→→▷Archive
→→→▷C1-ClownCake
→→→→▷(lots of picture files and details of the clown cake)
→→→▷C2-TrainCake
→→→→▷(train cake files)
→→→▷C3-EasterCake
→→→→▷(Easter cake files)
→→→▷C4-ClownCake
→→→→▷(second clown cake files)
→→▷Inuse
→→→▷C5-BirthdayCake
→→→→▷(which we are working on at the moment)

Doing it this way neatly separates our current areas of focus from finished things which are filed away. We'll work on that Birthday Cake, and when it's finished, move the folder over into the Archive.

Folders in Archive will occasionally be updated; older projects are occasionally tweaked or revisited, but generally things in Archive don't change much. When I take something out to modify or update, I tend to move it over into Inuse, do what I need to, then move it back when it's finished.

# CHAPTER 9

# CURRENT BUNS

# 9

Well, this is just about everything you could ever need, but there is one more type of folder I often use that you might find useful too. Like the 'Temporary' folders, I have lots of these and they are all named 'Current'.

The Current folders are used for various files, resources that I find useful on a regular basis. My 'Images → Current' folder, for example, has an image library and templates for social media headers. My 'Text → Current' folder includes letterheads, and my 'Videos → Current' folder includes video-effect scripts and templates for subtitles.

My Current folders include anything that I use quite often and which change quite often, so they are a bit more active than the archives, but are in constant use, unlike the Temporary folders which are only used in brief spurts.

I have a Current folder in Audio (this, incidentally, is where my MP3 Player files are), one in Images, one in Text, and one in Video.

Why are these different from any other general folder you might have? Well, they're not really, but because I use them more often I know that these are going to change regularly. 'Images → Current' has evolved to contain things generally useful for Images, but yes, I could create an 'Images → Clipart' folder and use that instead.

My 'Text → Current' folder is my most active folder. This contains Accounts; Manuals in '.pdf' format of everything in the house from my camera to the washing machine; current Bus Timetables; and the indices/diaries of my catalogued items like Artworks, Albums, and Books (and would contain the Master Cake Index, if I designed cakes).

CURRENT BUNS

# HOW TO

# CHAPTER 10

# BACKING UP

# 10

Sooner or later, your computer will become old. Its screen will start to flicker and stutter. Its hard drive will start to click and whirr, the light will stay on for what seems to be too long, and files will take longer than they should to load. These are signs of computer illness, and are, unfortunately, inevitable. I've become good at making backups because I've experienced a lot of lost data.

Regular backups have a dual purpose: to preserve your important data in case of a dramatic system failure, and to instil a regular cleaning routine to keep everything neat. Like our homes and lives, everything on our computers will start to get messy over time and, cliché though it sounds, there really is no substitute for manually checking through your computer and ensuring that everything is in order. No matter how neat things begin, or how diligent we are on a day-to-day basis, things will need regular checking, tidying, maintenance. So, for me, the word 'backup' means both making a copy of our latest data, and going through everything to tidy it, a virtual dusting of our room.

## Media City

The principle of a backup is to make an exact copy of our tree of files on an external system. Let's look at media options and how best to do it:

## 1. Hard drives.

Our computers have large hard drives so the simplest and most obvious way to back everything up is to copy everything to a second hard drive. Portable external hard drives tend to be very reliable, and relatively inexpensive. You can use an external 'caddy' or docking station which allows you to plug an internal hard drive directly into it and access it as though it were external.

One thing to avoid is to simply copy your files over to a new folder or alternative partition of your current hard drive because if your hard drive or computer should suffer a catastrophe, you might lose your original files and the backup too. A backup is for security, so it should ideally be as physically distant from the original machine as is convenient. If you have a large desktop computer, backing-up data to a second hard drive installed in the machine is a bad idea for this reason; a failure may destroy both things at once.

Hard drives are fantastically reliable, but remember that they are very delicate. They store their data using magnetism so must be protected from electric and magnetic fields like speakers and motors, and electric shocks. Hard drives are very sensitive to physical shocks too; one drop onto a hard surface can destroy them instantly, so they must be handled very delicately, as though made of the finest glass. Note that 'solid-state' hard drives, SSDs, are not hard drives but Flash Memory in a hard drive shape, so the information here about hard drives doesn't apply to those.

Despite these downsides, the size, speed, cost, reliability of external hard drives makes these the current best option for backups. As an ideal your hard drive would be stored in a metal, fire-proof and water-proof safe, cradled with soft, earthquake and bomb-proof wrapping, in a cave somewhere deep underground; so protected from electro-magnetic fields and global disasters; and you'll have a second or third copy in another building. If this ideal can't be met, and it rarely can, a metal cash-box and some bubble wrap will be good protection.

## 2. The Cloud

Cloud (or online) storage is a good option, but it can have downsides. Firstly, free storage is limited in size and anything above this will require a regular monthly payment. This can easily become a bill for life. What will become of your data if you skip a payment for a month? Or when you die? It will probably be deleted and lost forever.

Secondly, it can take a large amount of internet time to upload, download, and generally maintain your data; the cloud is a lot slower than a hard drive.

Thirdly, there is the issue of security. A hacker, or a colleague, could steal or delete your data, whether deliberately or accidentally. Finally, your data is in the hands of a distant company which may liquidate/go bust, change its Terms & Conditions concerning its use of your data, or lose or delete everything you've uploaded without warning.

The good things about cloud-based data is that it is stored far away, adding an extra level of protection from a local disaster, and usually free when using a small amount. Small amounts are the best size to upload and download, too. This makes cloud storage ideal when used for small amounts of very important data as a backup of last resort.

## 3. Optical Storage

CDs and DVDs have some advantages over hard drives in that they are small and easily transported, shock resistant, and immune to electromatic disturbances; so in the event of a nuclear war or extreme solar catastrophe which wipes out the world's hard drives, you, with your CD-ROM backups, would have the last laugh. The data is stored and read via pigments which deteriorate in the light and, much more slowly, naturally over time. Surface scratches can deteriorate the disks. You can purchase CD-R media which is certified to last 100 years. The two biggest disadvantages to CD-R or DVD-R as backup media are size; these tend be small, an archival CD-R holds 700MB; and the risk of obsolescence, as these media are becoming less and less popular.

Still, if you have a CD-R drive, then storing one or two disks of your most important data every so often will add an extra layer of security to your backups. To counter obsolescence, you could store a drive with the disks.

## 4. Flash Memory Devices

USB sticks, SD Cards, solid-state hard drives, and similar 'non-volatile memory' media have no moving parts, and in effect store their data using static electricity. These devices have grown larger, faster, and cheaper with each passing year since their invention. You can now buy a small plastic stick that can hold an entire computer's worth of data for far less than a clunky, mechanical hard-drive.

Flash memory devices are small and portable, physically sturdy, and reliable, but they have downsides. They can be slow to read and write from, and they naturally degrade over time in two ways: they have a limited number of write cycles, sort of like becoming more grainy with each save; and, even if unused in a drawer, they will gradually forget things bit by bit, their electric cloud fizzing away into mindless space. Most devices are certified for many years, 10 or more, and many thousands of write cycles.

The low price and large size of these make them good for backups, but don't rely on them as a sole backup for long term storage.

## The Last Word

Generally, when it comes to backups, it's better to have a few in different places on different media because no solution is perfect.

# Backup Routines

I complete regular backups every month, a second set every three months, and a third set every year. This means that, at any moment, I have three copies of my system of different ages. Sometimes the most recent backup is actually less reliable than an older one because things will accidentally be deleted or over-written.

Here are some tips for your backup routine:

### 1. Establish a regular time and date to perform a backup.

I backup on the first of each month. Anything slower than this, for me, would make the job take a lot longer. If you lost your computer today, how up to date would you like your most recent backup to be?

### 2. Compare.

On backup day, open two windows: your tree of files, and a second one of your backup. Set both views to look the same, so that you can easily flick between your computer and your backup to instantly see what is different.

### 3. Tidy.

Move through each folder to see what is new and different. Is anything in the wrong place? Does anything need renaming or deleting or changing? If things look fine, copy over anything that has changed since last time.

**4. Establish a system of knowing what is new and needs copying over, and what isn't.**

For my monthly backups, I'll copy over anything filed by date for the most recent month. This is one advantage of filing by date. For anything not filed by date, make your Operating System sort your folders by 'Date Modified', then you can see what has changed since last month.

That should catch every change, but it only works if you move through every folder you have, and if the computer really does know the date of when you modified those folders.

## MODIFYING DATES

This depends on your Operating System, but changes to a folder's contents generally resets that folder's date and time, and changes to the contents of any folders inside won't; so the 'Date Modified' of a folder is not an infallible record of its contents actually changing.

So, if you have something filed in 'Images → Cakes', a change to the contents of 'Cakes' will change the Date Modified of the Cakes folder, but not affect the Date Modified of 'Images'.

If you want to manually reset the Images date, rename Cakes to something (Cakes-X?) then rename it back. That will reset the Date Modified of Images.

For anything more complex that you might forget, usually some older thing (like toying around with documents from 2004...) make a note somewhere, a text file perhaps, of what you need to copy over during the next backup.

# X Marks The Ex

When copying over an existing folder, any new files will be added, and any existing files with an identical name will be replaced, but files in the destination that aren't in the source won't be deleted; so copying a new folder over an old one won't make the old one match the new one. How annoying. We need to exactly duplicate new over old.

The easiest way to do this is to delete the old folder then copy the new one, but this is a bit risky because you're deleting a backup before copying.

A better way to do this is to rename the old folder, then copy the new one over, then delete the old one. Not only is this safer, but it opens the door to keeping historical backups rather than deleting them at all. Here is an example:

Let's say you have folder 'Plants' and want to copy this over the older 'Plants' folder in your backups:

1. Rename the destination 'Plants-X'.
2. Copy over the source folder. The destination now contains 'Plants' and 'Plants-X'.
3. Delete Plants-X.

Easy peasy. After deleting, and assuming that your Operating System has a Recycle Bin, the 'Plants-X' will be in there, so you can identify it as the older version and restore it if you should need to.

X here means ex, as in older, but we use a single letter because we could, if we wanted, simply keep the folder and not delete it at all. When making a copy next time, we can then add another X to indicate an even older version, and so on, keeping a record of new, older, older still, and so on. These will be filed alphabetically, one after another, giving us a visual tree of most recent to oldest.

▷Plants
▷Plants-X
▷Plants-XX

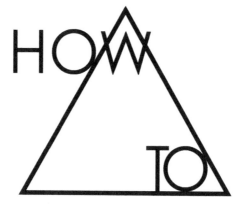

# CHAPTER 11

# RULES, AND BREAKING THEM

# 11

Sound the trumpets! You should now have all of the information you need to create a computer-world of order. In this last chapter, I thought I'd visit and revisit a few rules and, purely optional, guidelines.

We will start by revisiting the Golden Rule Number 1.

Remember this?:

## A folder should contain <u>only</u> files or <u>only</u> folders.

This is almost always a good idea. If you have a mix of files and folders, see if you can create a folder and put the loose files in there.

But, alas, there are some circumstances where you must (and will have to) break this rule. Programs usually have the main executable file (and other files it might use) in a main folder, and store other data in sub-folders. This is because programs often want to access hundreds of files and it would be confusing to put them all in one lump. Websites often do this too; the main index is usually in the root, but other pages (and images), are often in sub-folders. Microsoft Windows itself breaks the Golden Rule. The Windows folder is packed with lots of files AND lots of folders. Messy, but we have to live with it.

And now I present something of a style guide. These guidelines are optional, but I find them useful, so I thought I'd share them in case you do, too.

**1. Avoid spaces, dots, commas, and underscores in filenames. Capitalise the first letter of words. Use hyphens as separators.**

Use:
'MyTreePoems-Final.odt'
Not:
'mytreepoemsfinal.odt'
'My Tree Poems_Final.odt'
'MYTREE,Poems_Final.odt'

I find this makes filenames more readable, and that it's easier to identify a filename at a glance. Always keep extensions ('.odt') visible for this reason, too.

**2. Pad zeros when with four or fewer digits, else just use plain numbers.**

Use:
Image0001.jpg
Image0012.jpg

If you will have between 1 and 10,000 Images.

Avoid lots of zeros, like 'Image00000001.jpg' because too many in a row become hard to count at a glance. If in doubt, or if you think it looks neater, forget about padding and use:

Image1.jpg
Image12.jpg
etc.

## 3. Use 'v' followed by a three-digit version number, to indicate version.

Before we start I will admit that this is a bit of an arbitrary rule of personal choice, but I find it really useful to name files with a version. For a finished document, I put 'v100' at the end, which means 'version 1.00'. For unfinished work in progress I use 'v001', 'v002' etc.

For each update I add 1, so 'MyFile-v100.txt' becomes 'MyFile-v101.txt', then 'MyFile-v102.txt', as times goes on.

This will give you 1000 possible updates to your file.

'MyTreePoems-v001.odt'
becomes
'MyTreePoems-v002.odt'
then
'MyTreePoems-v100.odt'
when considered finished, and
'MyTreePoems-v101.odt'
when updated a notch.

This 'vxxx' code is bound more by a desire for neatness and utility, than logic. A lot of software in particular uses three version numbers: major, minor, and tiny. The e-book editor Calibre, for example, has a version '5.13.0' - which is already beyond what my 3-digit code can cope with. We could use 6 digits - 2 for major, 2 minor, 2 tiny, but I don't really want to have files like 'MyPoems-v051300.txt' - this looks a bit long and complicated. Neatness and ease should be our goal.

But I do find it useful to know what version a file is at a glance, particularly with written documents, and the software I develop. I only use these when a file is likely to be updated, and when I want to see which version I have – I don't put 'v100' on everything. This book, as I write it, is a prime example. I can see which is the latest version, and keep a few older versions, just in case. If I send a copy to someone or upload a copy somewhere, I'll know what version they have, and it's easy to save out a copy with a new version number at any time, if I think it's been updated enough.

## 4. Use text files as reminders to yourself.

There are always judgement choices to be made, and often an item can fit into several categories. I store my programming documentation in 'Programming', but it could logically be in 'Text → Manuals', too.

It's important to avoid a copy of the same thing in two different locations because one thing can be changed or updated, leaving the other obsolete or wrong, and you can bet that you'll accidentally find and use the wrong one.

One tip is to file things once, and in a possible second place, put a small file or pointer, a manual short-cut. This is a text file and can be named to point you in the right direction eg. 'See Cakes.txt'[1], so that you can see at a glance where you should be looking. If a filename isn't enough information, I create a file called 'ReadMe.txt' and in the file itself I'll type details inside of where to find what I want. I use these ReadMe files to remind myself how to file things, too, if I need reminding of a particularly complicated system of what goes where and in what format.

## 5. Rules

Looking through my 20+ years of computer files, and 20+ years of filing and organising, I can see that I don't really use any more guidelines than that, but you can glean some more information about how I write dates, and file my master indices in the Appendices.

The final rule is that all good rules can be broken at times.[2]

Let ease of use and ease of reading be your ultimate guide. As archivists, we must be agile and adaptable, as well as consistent and neat.

### NOTES

1. Yes, I've added spaces in the filename. As a note to me, I've made ease of me reading it a priority.
2. See 1.

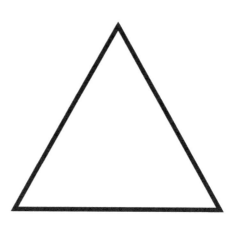

APPENDICES

# A1

# Appendix 1: Diary Indexing

When I index my creations I tend to use plain text. I could use a spreadsheet, or a database, or umpteen other things, but I like the freedom to type a lot of notes, like a diary, about each project. Over the years, this way of working has become invaluable because the analytical aspect of writing about a project in an easy way has allowed me to improve, learn and grow as I create, and all as a natural side-effect of having a catalogue.

Here is an example entry in the format I use, for the Clown Cake in our example:

```
C1 Clown Cake (code and name)
Date Filed
25 Dec 2010
Recipe
(any recipe details)
Chronology
4 Jul 2009: Mused about making a clown cake.
1 Dec 2010: Bought cherries.
10 Dec 10:00-10:45: Main baking.
20 Dec: Final decoration.
Notes
My clown cake, which I'd dreamed about making
for years. In late December 2010, I finally
got baking. Other various notes go here.
```

So, we have 'Date Filed', which can be the final completion date of the cake, or any sort of reference date you like (Start Date, Finish Date, whatever you like, provided it is consistent).

The 'Chronology' field is common to most of my projects. I don't always update it, but it's often useful to know what you did when. Remember, this information will be of greatest use to you in the distant future when you've forgotten how and when and why you made this cake. The more you store, the more useful your diary will be.

I've added 'Recipe' here but you can invent as many fields or things to store as you like. These will be specific for each project. For my oil paintings I include the colours I use. For my music albums, I include track lists, song links, ISRC codes and that sort of thing.

Here is one of my actual Artwork Index entries as a working example:

```
G640 An Experience That Isn't Shared Is The
Same As No Experience
Date Filed
17 Nov 2013
Variant A: Original.
Format: Oil on medium density fibreboard, size
470x368x6mm, visible area 420x318mm. Medium
density fibreboard (purchased B&Q 2013). Sawn.
Front, rear, and edges painted with Golden
GAC100 100% Acrylic Dispersion Polymer
(purchased 2013). The front was then painted
with several thin layers of Winsor and Newton
Acrylic Gesso Primer pigmented with titanium
white (purchased 2009).
Days work
5
Extra Costs
£30 = £30 (Outer Frame)
```

APPENDICES

Medium Used (Imprimatura)
Three parts Winsor and Newton Sansodor low
odour solvent to one part Spectrum Alkaflow.
Colours Used (Imprimatura)
BX french ultramarine deep.
Colours Used (Underpainting)
Sky: BX french ultramarine, WN mars black, MH
titanium white, BX mars violet.
Sea: BX cobalt turquoise green, BX cobalt
turquoise blue, WN cobalt turquoise light, BX
french ultramarine, WN mars black, MH titanium
white, BX mars violet.
Boat: MH naples yellow, BX mars violet, BX
nickel yellow, WN mars black, MH titanium
white.
Earth: MH naples yellow, BX mars violet, BX
nickel yellow, BX cobalt turquoise green, BX
cobalt turquoise blue, BX french ultramarine,
WN mars black, MH titanium white.
Monolith: MH naples yellow, BX light red, BX
mars violet, BX nickel yellow, BX cobalt
turquoise green, BX cobalt turquoise blue, WN
mars black, MH titanium white.
Medium Used (Layer 1)
One part Winsor and Newton Stand Oil, two
parts James Grove's Amber Varnish, nine parts
Robertsons Refined Safflower Oil, drops of
Baldwins Spike Lavender Oil.
Colours Used (Layer 1)
Sky: BX ultramarine deep, MH raw umber, BX
manganese violet, MH titanium white.
Sea: BX ultramarine deep, BX viridian, MH
titanium white, WN burst sienna, WN
transparent maroon.
Monolith: WN yellow ochre light, WN
transparent red ochre, BX ultramarine deep, BX
viridian, WN burst sienna, MH raw umber.
Boat: WN yellow ochre light, BX ultramarine

deep, WN burst sienna, MH raw umber.
Published Editions
A: Original.
Chronology
20 Aug 2013: Concept.
27 Aug: Modelling and photography.
2 Sep: Sketched.
4 Sep: Traced to panel.
7 Sep: Imprimatura applied.
1 Oct: Underpainting.
9 Nov: Layer 1: Sky, planet.
17 Nov: Layer 1: Sea, boat, monolith.
22 Mar 2014: Frame stained.
Notes
An idea inspired by a Facebook mention by
Jamie, saying about how you make your own
family, after he'd had a day out with his. I
felt alone, and felt the relative unimportance
of an experience only one person experiences,
so decided to try to represent that. The
violet sky presented a challenge I relished.
Difficult because of transparency of these
hues, I used grey tinted with ultramarine to
create a relatively neutral backdrop. For the
sea, the cobalt turquoise colours created a
strong chrominance similar to the mock-up. I
used a different reference image of the planet
Earth to good effect, and took time painting
the boat. I wasn't happy with it but it was on
par with the source image from one version of
Böcklin's Isle of the Dead. I used lots of
colours for the monolith. For the frame I
envisaged a dark box with a golden frame, like
the Tiger Moving Nowhere. After time I thought
that dark violet would be better than pure
black, and so first stained a pine frame of my
own construction with a mix of GFA Raw Umber
and water, then water and GFA Dioxazine.

*An Experience That Isn't Shared is the Same as No Experience*
Oil on medium density fibreboard, 42.0 x 31.8 cm

# A2

# Appendix 2: Readable Date Format

The ISO standard for dates uses YYYY-MM-DD format. A forward slash is used to bridge from/to dates. In ISO format, the dates from 3rd to 19th February 2012 would read '2012-02-03/2012-02-19'. This is very logical but I don't find it very readable.

For my written dates and times in text files I use a standard or my own, which I thought I would share in case you find this useful. This can cover a specific date and time, or a span of dates or times.

The format is: day, month as three-letter indicator, year. The word 'to' connects a range of dates, and the 'from' date omits months or years which remain the same. Month letters should be specified if a lone day number would otherwise be present, to avoid ambiguous solitary numbers.

For example:

19 Nov 2012
Equates to 19th of November 2012.

3 to 19 Nov 2012
Equates the 3rd of November 2012 to the 19th of November 2012.

3 Oct to 19 Nov 2012
Equates to 3rd of October 2012 to 19th of November 2012.

3 Oct 2011 to 19 Feb 2012
Equates to 3rd of October 2011 to 19th of February 2012.

Times should be 24-hour format:

5 Oct 10:00 to 10 Oct 2013 18:00
Equates to a five day range, from 10am on 5th October to 6pm on 10th October 2013.

Time ranges are separated with a hyphen from–to and are assumed to apply to all dates in a range.

5 to 10 Oct 2013 10:00–14:00
Equates to a five day range, each day active from 10am to 2pm.

Semicolons are used to separate specific days rather than a range:
3 Oct; 6 Oct; 9 Oct 2011

10 Oct 2013 10:00–14:00; 16:00–18:00
Will indicate two time periods on 10th October 2013.

10 to 15 Oct 10:00–22:00; 17 Oct 2013 10:30–22:00
To indicate periods over several dates with different times.

When I list activities per line, I list the year in question first and always include the month:

1 Mar 2009 10:00–16:00: Today is the 1st of March, from 10am to 4pm.

12 Mar: Today is the 12th of March 2009.
5 Jan 2010: It's January now.
5 Feb: It's 5th Feb 2010 today.

Other written works by Mark Sheeky

## as Author

365 Universes, Pentangel Books (2012)
The Many Beautiful Worlds of Death, Pentangel Books (2015)
Deep Dark Light, Pentangel Books (2018)
21st Century Surrealism, Pentangel Books (2018)
The Burning Circus, Pentangel Books (2019)
The Intangible Man & Other Strange Tales, Pentangel Books (2020)

## as Illustrator

Songs Of Life, Pentangel Books (2014)
Testing the Delicates, Ink Pantry Publishing (2017)
Wilkommen Zum Rattenfänger Theater, Ink Pantry Publishing (2019)
Solitary Child Friend of Immortals, Ink Pantry Publishing (2020)
Super8 Magicscape, Ink Pantry Publishing (2021)

## as Contributor

Hide It!, Mardibooks (2014)
The Ball of the Future, Earlyworks Press (2015)
Journeys Beyond, Earlyworks Press (2015)
Diversifly, Fair Acre Press (2018)

## www.marksheeky.com